Let's Pretend!

Written by Kate Scott

Illustrated by Ashley Stewart

Collins

T0364541

Dev dipped his toe into the pool, checking it wasn't too cold.

Jake slid in. "Jump in!" he called to Dev, poking his head out of the waves he'd made.

Dev splashed his way over to Jake. "Let's pretend we're swimming in the sea," he said.

Dev and Jake swam down. Jake pointed in front of him, "Look over there! A sea snake!"

"What's that?" asked Dev.

"It's a cave," said Jake. "Let's take a look inside."

They entered the mystical cave.

"I can't see," said Jake feeling his way in the dark.

Jake screamed. His hand was entwined in a veil of seaweed.

Together the boys lifted the seaweed,
to find a colossal ...

"SQUID!" Dev screamed. "Swim for your life!"

10

The boys swam out of the cave as fast as they could.

"It's got my costume!" Jake called.

Dev swam back to help Jake.

Dev needed a plan, fast. He grabbed the seaweed and wound it round and round the squid.

Now the squid couldn't see. As it tugged at the seaweed it let go of Jake.

"Quick! Swim!" Dev shouted.

Both boys swam away from the squid. They swam faster and faster. They didn't dare look back.

They swam past sea snakes, flounders,

a manta ray and seals.

They didn't stop until they had reached the top.

"Hooray! That was fun!" cheered Dev.
Jake said, "Let's pretend next week, too!"

Dev's mum called, "Come on, Dev!"
Jake's mum called, "Come on, Jake!"

Pretending

After reading

Letters and Sounds: Phase 5

Word count: 247

Focus phonemes: /oa/ oe, o /ai/ a-e, ay, ei, ey /e/ ea /ee/ ea /u/ o /igh/ i-e, i/i/ y /oo/ oul /oo/ u-e /oi/ oy /ar/ a /ow/ ou /ear/ eer /air/ are, ere /or/ al /u/ o-e /o/ a

Common exception words: of, to, the, into, my, he, we (we're), said, what (what's)

Curriculum links: Science: Animals, including humans

National Curriculum learning objectives: Spoken language: use relevant strategies to build their vocabulary; use spoken language to develop understanding through speculating, hypothesising, imagining and exploring ideas; Reading/word reading: read other words of more than one syllable that contain taught GPCs; Reading/ comprehension: understand both the books they can already read accurately and fluently and those they listen to by making inferences on the basis of what is being said and done; be encouraged to link what they read or hear read to their own experiences

Developing fluency

- Your child may enjoy hearing you read the book.
- Play the part of one of the characters and ask your child to play the other part. Read the dialogue on pages 6 and 7, miming actions and using lots of expression.
- Now do the same with pages 10 and 11.

Phonic practice

- Ask your child to sound out each of the following words:

  ch/e/ck   h/ea/d

- Ask your child:
  - Can you tell me which sound is the same in each word? (/e/)
  - Can you point to the grapheme (letter or letters) that represent the /e/ sound in each word? (*e, ea*)
- Can you think of any other words with the /e/ sound in them? (e.g. *bed, bread*)

Extending vocabulary

- Read the following sets of words to your child. Can they spot the odd one out in each set?

1.	colossal	huge	tiny	gigantic	(*tiny*)
2.	veil	mask	back	cover	(*back*)
3.	screamed	whispered	shouted	shrieked	(*whispered*)
4.	slow	quick	speedy	fast	(*slow*)